TALLCHIEF
America's Prima Ballerina

by Maria Tallchief with Rosemary Wells
illustrations by Gary Kelley

PUFFIN BOOKS

PUFFIN BOOKS
Published by the Penguin Group
Penguin Putnam Books for Young Readers, 345 Hudson Street, New York, New York 10014, U.S.A.
Penguin Books Ltd, 27 Wrights Lane, London W8 5TZ, England
Penguin Books Australia Ltd, Ringwood, Victoria, Australia
Penguin Books Canada Ltd, 10 Alcorn Avenue, Toronto, Ontario, Canada M4V 3B2
Penguin Books (N.Z.) Ltd, 182-190 Wairau Road, Auckland 10, New Zealand

Penguin Books Ltd, Registered Offices: Harmondsworth, Middlesex, England

First published in the United States of America by Viking, a division of Penguin Putnam Books for Young Readers, 1999
Published by Puffin Books, a division of Penguin Putnam Books for Young Readers, 2001
21

THE LIBRARY OF CONGRESS HAS CATALOGED THE VIKING EDITION AS FOLLOWS:
Tallchief, Maria.
Tallchief: American's prima ballerina / by Maria Tallchief with Rosemary Wells; pictures by Gary Kelley.—1st ed.
p. cm.
Summary: Ballerina Maria Tallchief describes her childhood on an Osage reservation,
the development of her love of dance, and her rise to success in that field.
ISBN 0-670-88756-0
1. Tallchief, Maria—Juvenile literature. 2. Ballerinas—United States—Biography—Juvenile literature.
3. Osage Indians—United States—Biography—Juvenile Literature. [1. Tallchief, Maria. 2. Ballet dancers.
3. Osage Indians—Biography. 4. Indians of North America—Biography. 5. Women—Biography.]
I. Wells, Rosemary. II. Kelley, Gary, ill. III. Title.
GV1785.T32A3 1999 792'.028'092 [B]—DC21 98-35783 CIP AC

Puffin Books ISBN 978-0-14-230018-3

Printed in China

Maria Tallchief is a charming and down-to-earth person. At the time of this writing she is almost seventy-five years old, but she moves as gracefully as a woman of twenty. She was the greatest American-born ballerina of her time. Her most famous roles were in *Firebird*, *Swan Lake*, and other classical ballets. She was married to the great choreographer George Balanchine, who created many roles for her. She performed all over the world. Her speed and strength of movement were so exciting to watch that she electrified the world of dance.

Here is how I came to write this book with her.

When I was little and had been good and my hands were very, very clean, my mother would open a locked bureau drawer and allow me to run my fingers over the fronts of six silk blouses that the legendary ballerina Anna Pavlova had given her. The blouses had sparkling buttons and labels from Hermes in Paris. My mother had been a member of the corps de ballet of the Ballets Russes de Monte Carlo when Pavlova was dancing with them.

My mother was never a great dancer. "There was only one great American dancer," she used to tell me. "Tallchief." She told me once of a trip to California in 1938. She had snapshots of herself and the company, in dark woolen belted bathing suits, stacked up like acrobats on Malibu Beach without a house in sight. She told me about the amazing groves of orange trees and about the funny little dirt-road town that was Los Angeles.

In our lives there are many unexplained circles of happenstance no heavier than light. When I found out that my mother was somewhere on the stage when Maria Tallchief, sixteen years old, saw the Russian ballet for the first time, I decided it was time to write this book with Maria, herself.   R. W.

*I*was born on an Osage Indian Reservation in Fairfax, Oklahoma, in the year 1925.

My father, Alexander Tallchief, was a full-blooded Osage, and he looked just like the Indian on the buffalo-head nickel. He could spot a rattlesnake out of the corner of his eye, aim his rifle, and shoot the snake from fifty yards away while still walking.

My father had never known the life of his ancestors. He told me that when he was a boy, oil was discovered on the Osage land in Fairfax. In a short time the oil fields would produce more riches than all the gold rushes in history. The Osage people owned the head rights to the oil on their land, and their lives changed forever when the black fountains of "Oklahoma crude" came out of the ground.

I was told that the Osage people were the wealthiest people on the face of the earth. This was true. Osage men wore beads woven into the cloth of their trousers. Osage women sewed semiprecious stones into belts and jewelry. My father had a long red Pierce Arrow car, which he loved to show off up and down the main street of Fairfax.

My mother, Ruth Porter, was a Scots-Irish woman whose people had settled in Oklahoma when it became a state. Her people had been pioneers from Scotland and had fought their way west in covered wagons a hundred years before. In character she was the opposite of my handsome, playful father. She was small as a bird, and beautiful. My father loved to give her diamond rings.

My name is Elizabeth Marie Tallchief. I was born with music that flowed through my body as naturally as blood in my veins. This was a gift from God. I became a pioneer for American dance, and this was a gift from my mother.

My mother was proud of our brick house high on the hill among the cottonwoods and blackjack oak trees. She tended house and family for my father. She taught my sister, Marjorie, and me right from wrong and everything in between. But more than any other thing, my mother heard the music that was born along with me like a second heart.

Those of us born with music or poems or colors inside always know it right away. I would only have to hear a melody, and out it came from the piano keys under my fingers, or in dance.

Mother found a piano teacher and a dance teacher for Marjorie and me.

I practiced long hours of *First Piano Exercises* in the cool of our tile-roofed house under the baking sun. Then I would pick out the tunes I loved from the radio.

The secret of music is that it is something like a house with many rooms. My first simple exercises were like the frame of a house before it is built. The frame of good music has to be strong enough to hold the weight of a whole symphony, and delicate enough to break the heart.

Perched on three books and a pillow at our piano I learned this, but not in words. I learned it in the way you learn the smell of bread in the oven or the color of leaves in the fall. The truth of this came to me easily, because it was all there in the music itself.

Our dance teacher, Mrs. Sabin, was not a good teacher and had no idea how to prepare two youngsters for a professional life on the stage. But she did what she could. She dreamed up routines and programs. I performed "Glow Little Glow Worm" before an audience at a rodeo.

At the county fair I danced to "The Stars and Stripes Forever." Banging away on a badly tuned piano, Mrs. Sabin directed me and conducted an imaginary orchestra while I twirled and leaped in my mother's cut-to-size negligees decorated with feathers and ropes of fake pearls. Mrs. Sabin had Marjorie and me dance on point, the tips of the toes, which is something no good teacher asks a very young child to do.

Among my father's people women do not dance—only the men. In those days it was illegal for Indians to live in any way but the white man's way. Dancing and other native ceremonies were considered "bad for us." White men believed that the religious ceremonies of our people would keep us in primitive ignorance forever.

Our culture and language were against the law, but we didn't care. What the government said didn't matter a fig to us. Our drums went on as they always had. To this day I remember their rhythm.

My grandmother Tallchief allowed us to watch the forbidden dances of the Osage people. These ceremonies were held in hidden places known only to the tribal members. They dressed in blankets, beads, and silver jewelry, and sat in circles smoking pipes, watching and talking. They never looked at the person to whom they were speaking, but preferred to feel their presence instead.

I was unlike most of the children on the reservation, because I spent so many hours at the piano and going to dance lessons. I had a cousin, Pearl, who lived with my grandmother Tallchief. Pearl was an orphan and would one day inherit her father and mother's oil lands. This wispy Pearl, Oklahoma dust between her toes, might have been one of the richest people in the United States.

Pearl and her friends used to peek through our living room window. They giggled at my mother directing me at the piano.

One day Mother decided that Fairfax, Oklahoma, was not going to give us the education we needed. My father agreed. Mother told us it was time to move on. Like her pioneer ancestors we went west, not east. We went in my father's Pierce Arrow, not a Conestoga wagon. But still it was an adventure.

In the year 1933, America had no big highways, only small towns and little roads that wound on forever. We stayed in hotels with banging pipes and narrow stairways. We stayed in cabins that had no indoor plumbing at all. We ate bacon and eggs and hamburgers because mother said that was a reliable kind of meal anywhere you went.

We arrived in Los Angeles one day, tired and hungry. Before anything else, my father showed us the Pacific Ocean. I was terrified, never having imagined anything as threatening as this crashing, enormous water.

Then we went to lunch at a drugstore near Wilshire Boulevard. As we ate our hamburgers, Mother asked the clerk if there was a local ballet school. He told her where Mr. Belcher's School of Ballet was, and so we met our new teacher.

Daddy found us a house with palm trees and avocado plants in the backyard right there in the Wilshire District.

Mr. Belcher took me and Marjorie in hand. He told us that everything we had learned from Mrs. Sabin was wrong, and now we had to begin again.

He sat while he taught, and demonstrated all the steps and movements from his chair. He told us he had studied in England with the great Italian-Russian ballet master Enrico Cechetti at the turn of the last century.

My father woke me up each morning at six. I practiced piano from seven to eight. School went until three. After school there would be another hour of piano and then ballet or music lessons. Marjorie had the same day and loved it as much as I.

I did well in school and enjoyed my friends, but my days were full of practice. People asked, "Don't you get tired of all that practice, Betty Marie?" But I'd just say, "How can I get tired of what I love?"

When I was twelve I changed ballet schools and my life as a dancer really began. It began because my father said, "You must choose piano or dance, Betty Marie. One or the other, but follow that one star."

How did I choose this path over the other?

I chose dance because I felt the music I loved grew inside of me in a different way than could be expressed by my hands on an instrument. It coursed through my body.

If I chose piano I would have music but not dance. If I chose dance I would have both. In the way that very young people choose, from the heart, I chose, and I chose right.

I had a third gift, just as important as the first two, and that was a mother and father who allowed me to choose.

My new teacher, Madame Nijinska, said, "When you sleep, you must sleep like a dancer. When you stand and wait for the bus, you must wait for the bus like a dancer."

Madame Nijinska was as strict as a drill sergeant in the army. She had come from Russia and was very well-known there. She was the sister of Nijinsky, the most famous ballet dancer in the world. To us in Los Angeles, he was like a god, and so she was the sister of a god. Madame spoke little English, but managed to get every thought she wanted across to the pupils of her class.

We were not allowed to slouch or hang on the barre lazily. After we had finished an exercise, we had to walk to one side and stand with perfect posture until it was time for the next exercise.

We repeated steps over and over, learning how to balance, how to breathe properly, and how to hold a position so that all of our back muscles were in use. Elbows had to be held in a certain way. In first position, the little finger should touch the front of the thigh. If Madame came over and could move your elbow, the position was wrong and you had to do it until it was right. She taught us proper breathing. She taught us that what allowed her brother to fly like a bird and stay an extra two seconds in the air every time he leaped was his abdominal muscle control. This she explained as a dancer holding her soul in the middle of her body.

But more than any single thing, I remember she taught us how to listen to music. First the composer felt the emotions of the story he wanted to tell in music. He could hear the music in his head before it was played. He wrote it down as notes on paper. These emotions were interpreted by instruments of the orchestra. In turn, we as dancers had to listen to the composer's heart and soul by means of that music and express it all a third time in the movements of our bodies.

America was a much younger country at that time. It was so brash and new and full of hard physical work that it was only beginning to have time for music and painting and poetry. The great artists of the world were all still Europeans.

I had been to ballet performances in Los Angeles, but I had never seen the great dancers. They were all Russian. They belonged to a troupe called the Ballets Russes de Monte Carlo, and they came at last. They had been five days on the train trip from New York because no one flew in planes yet. In the 1930s the California air was clear and Los Angeles was a small town surrounded with orange groves. The dancers were ecstatic to be in our warm climate.

I went to every performance of the Ballets Russes. The whole company visited the studio and walked around like ordinary people, but to me they were angels from heaven. Alexandra Danilova, the star, gave Madame Nijinska roses and executed a reverence as she presented them.

I could not believe what was before my eyes. The Ballets Russes de Monte Carlo were a world in themselves. The dancers were as graceful and silky as birds of paradise.

They knew the names of ocean liners. Whispering or joking in Russian and French and English, they talked of long train rides in the night. I heard the names of theaters in Casablanca and Paris and Rome. They spoke easily of Russian princes and of the fate of Madame Pavlova's flock of swans that lived on the lawn of her house near London. I heard about the war coming and opera costumes lost in the station in Berlin. I wanted this life so very badly.

All I had to offer was my ability to speak the language of music. I knew how it was sung by a voice or played on a flute or piano, and how it was spoken by the body itself. That language I knew in the way I knew how to breathe the air.

What I needed to learn was how to be strong enough to dance for hours in a matinee and then do the whole thing perfectly again in the evening. And I needed to be delicate enough to break the human heart.

I spoke to my mother and father, and they agreed to let me go to New York to see about joining the Ballets Russes de Monte Carlo. When I was seventeen, Mother bought me a red gabardine suit and high heels to wear in New York. Daddy drove all of us to the station. Marjorie, still in high school, said good-bye. And I got on a train and joined the world of my angels, where there were ocean liners and the opera house in Paris, and people threw roses because we had made them so happy.